M000220053

the
baby owner's
maintenance log

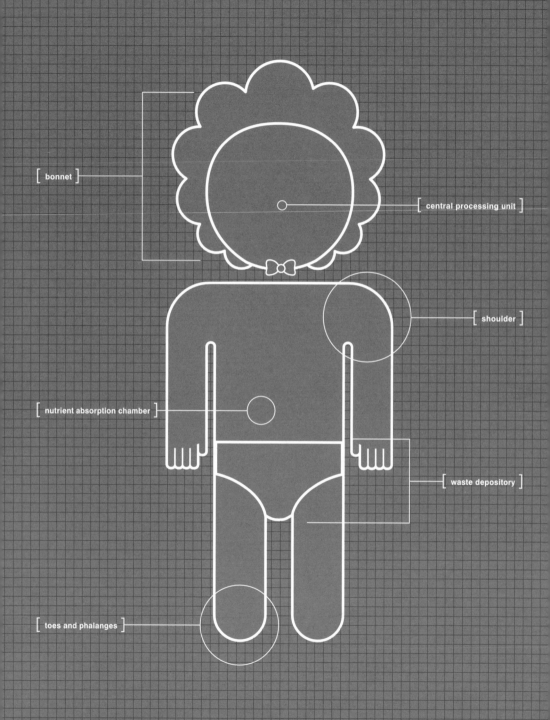

[bonnet]

[central processing unit]

[shoulder]

[nutrient absorption chamber]

[waste depository]

[toes and phalanges]

the
baby
owner's maintenance log

A RECORD OF YOUR MODEL'S FIRST YEAR

by Louis Borgenicht, M.D., and Joe Borgenicht, D.A.D.,
with Lynn Rosen, M.O.M.

Illustrated by Paul Kepple and Jude Buffum

W0010438

QUIRK BOOKS
PHILADELPHIA

ALSO AVAILABLE

THE BABY OWNER'S MANUAL

ISBN 1-931686-23-8

LOUIS BORGENICHT, M.D., is a board-certified pediatrician with the American Academy of Pediatrics and has worked for the last 16 years at his private practice in Salt Lake City, Utah. He was named "best pediatrician in Utah" by *Ladies' Home Journal* in 2001. He is the co-author of *The Baby Owner's Manual*.

JOE BORGENICHT, D.A.D., is a father who frequently telephones his dad for advice. He's the co-author of *The Baby Owner's Manual* and *The Action Hero's Handbook*.

Copyright © 2004 by Quirk Productions, Inc. • Illustrations copyright © 2004 by Headcase Design

All rights reserved. No part of this book may be reproduced in any form without written permission from the publisher.

ISBN 1-931686-25-4

Printed in Malaysia • Typeset in Swiss

Designed by Paul Kepple and Jude Buffum @ Headcase Design

Distributed in North America by Chronicle Books • 85 Second Street • San Francisco, CA 94105
10 9 8 7 6 5 4 3 2 1

Quirk Books • 215 Church Street • Philadelphia, PA 19106 • www.quirkbooks.com

Contents

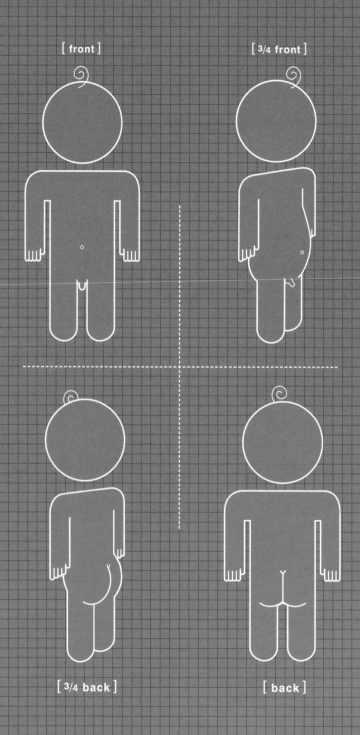

[front]   [3/4 front]

[3/4 back]   [back]

Welcome
to Your New Baby!

Congratulations on the arrival of your new baby.

This baby is surprisingly similar to other appliances you may already own. Like a personal computer, for instance, the baby will require a source of power to execute her many complicated tasks and functions. Like a videocassette recorder, the baby's head will require frequent cleanings for optimum performance. And like an automobile, the baby may expel unpleasant odors into the atmosphere.

When used properly, the baby will provide years of love, devotion, and joy. Record every significant change in your model's behavior or programming here in *The Baby Owner's Maintenance Log*. Note everything from the first use of the vocal system to the tiny baby acne that crops up. This log is your workbook and scrapbook for tracking and remembering all the notable events of your model's first year.

At three months, six months, and twelve months, you'll find maintenance checklists to help you assess your model's progress. Of course, all models will activate different functions at different times—checklists are merely loose guidelines, not factory-specified requirements. You can use the checklists simply to note what functions are working, and when they started working. At the back of the log are charts for tracking waste functions, feeding, and sleep functioning. Store prescription slips, silly photographs, or even locks of hair in the convenient envelope.

Good luck—and enjoy your new baby!

Owner's Record

OWNER INFORMATION

○ Mr. ○ Mrs. ○ Ms.	First Name	Initial	Last Name
○ Mr. ○ Mrs. ○ Ms.	First Name	Initial	Last Name

Address (Number and Street)	Apt. #

City	State/Province	Zip/Postal Code

DATE MODEL ARRIVED

☐☐ / ☐☐ / ☐☐☐☐

Day   Month   Year

MODEL NAME

First Name	Middle Name	Last Name

MODEL NUMBERS

Weight	Length	Head Circumference	Apgar Score

NAME OF HOSPITAL WHERE DELIVERED

DOCTOR'S NAME

GENITAL APPARATUS

○ Male   ○ Female

HAIR

○ Yes   ○ No   ┊ If yes, color   ○ black   ○ blond   ○ brown   ○ red

EYE COLOR

○ blue   ○ brown   ○ gray   ○ green   ○ hazel

OTHER NOTABLE FEATURES

Did you purchase this item yourself, or was it a gift?

Your feelings and feedback upon receipt and inspection of model:

How many other similar products do you have in your house?

Name	Age	Name	Age
Name	Age	Name	Age

QUICK REFERENCE GUIDE

Virtually all current models come pre-installed with the following features and capabilities. If the baby

THE HEAD

HEAD: May initially appear unusually large or even cone-shaped, depending on model and delivery option. A cone-shaped head will become more rounded after four to eight weeks.

CIRCUMFERENCE: The average head circumference of all models is 13.8 inches (35 cm). Any measurement between 12.9 and 14.7 inches (32–37 cm) is considered normal.

HAIR: Not available upon delivery with every model. Color may vary.

FONTANELS (ANTERIOR AND POSTERIOR): Also known as "soft spots." Fontanels are two gaps in the baby's skull where the bones have not grown together. Never apply pressure to the fontanels. They should seal completely by the end of the first year (or soon after).

EYES: Most Caucasian models are delivered with blue or gray eyes, while African and Asian models are usually delivered with brown eyes. Be aware that the pigmentation of the iris may change several times during the first few months. The baby will automatically settle on an eye color by the age of nine to twelve months.

NECK: Upon arrival, this feature may appear "useless." This is not a defect. The neck will become more useful in two to four months.

...ssing one or more of the functions described herein, contact the baby's service provider immediately.

THE BODY

SKIN: The baby's skin may be exceptionally sensitive to the chemicals found in new (unwashed) garments. The skin may react poorly to the chemicals in ordinary laundry detergent. Consider switching to a fragrance-free, chemical-free detergent for all of the laundry in the household.

UMBILICAL STUMP: This appendage will become scabbed and, after several weeks, will fall off. It must be kept clean and dry to avoid infection and to form a healthy navel.

RECTUM: This is the site of the baby's solid waste output. A thermometer placed in this port will measure the baby's core temperature, which should be approximately 98.6 degrees Fahrenheit (37°C).

GENITALS: It is normal for the baby's genitals to appear slightly enlarged. This has no relation to the future size or shape of the baby's genitals.

FUZZ: Many models come pre-installed with lanugo, a downy coating of hair on the shoulders or back. This coating will disappear within a few weeks.

WEIGHT: The average model weighs 7.5 pounds (3.4 kg) on delivery. The majority weigh between 5.5 and 10 pounds (2.5–4.5 kg).

LENGTH: The average model is 20 inches (51 cm) long on delivery. The majority are between 18 and 22 inches (45–56 cm) long.

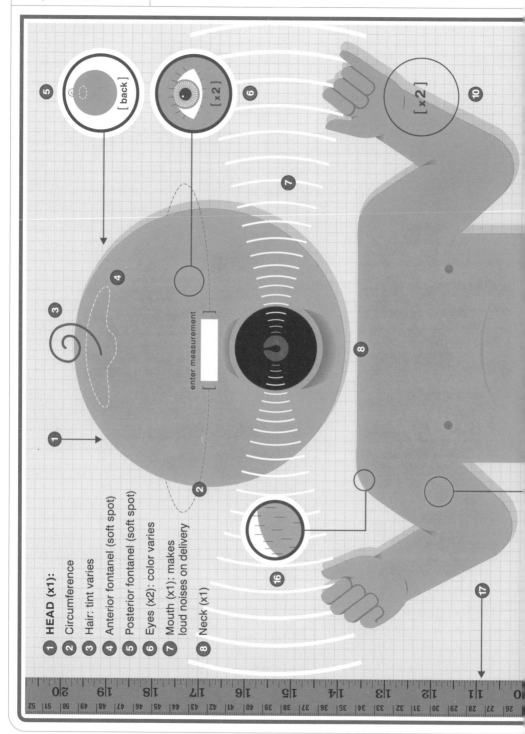

1 **HEAD (x1):**
2 Circumference
3 Hair: tint varies
4 Anterior fontanel (soft spot)
5 Posterior fontanel (soft spot)
6 Eyes (x2): color varies
7 Mouth (x1): makes loud noises on delivery
8 Neck (x1)

[back]

[x2]

[x2]

enter measurement

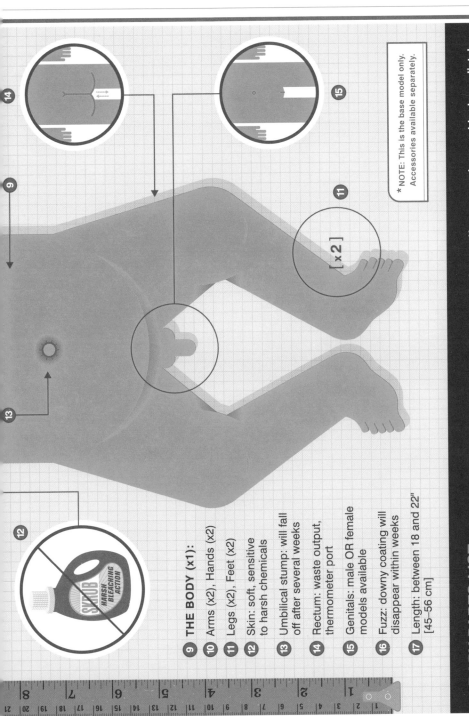

⑨ THE BODY (x1):

⑩ Arms (x2), Hands (x2)

⑪ Legs (x2), Feet (x2)

⑫ Skin: soft, sensitive to harsh chemicals

⑬ Umbilical stump: will fall off after several weeks

⑭ Rectum: waste output, thermometer port

⑮ Genitals: male OR female models available

⑯ Fuzz: downy coating will disappear within weeks

⑰ Length: between 18 and 22" [45–56 cm]

[x2]

HARSH BLEACHING ACTION SCRUB

* NOTE: This is the base model only. Accessories available separately.

BABY PARTS LIST: Check your model carefully. If any parts are missing, notify your service provider immediately.

All models come pre-installed with a complete set of features and capabilities. However, for technological reasons, all of these features do not function immediately. Please also note that each model is different and begins various functions at different stages in the life cycle of the equipment.

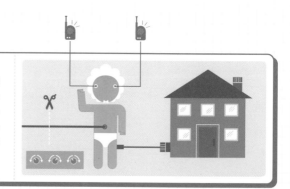

Upon delivery, all of the umbilical cord is removed except the stump at the location of attachment to the baby. Total removal at this stage would mar the surface of the model. In order to assure that your model is delivered in flawless condition, a tiny stump is left attached, which will dry up and fall off of its own accord within weeks, or even days, of delivery.

DATE WHEN BABY'S UMBILICAL CORD FELL OFF   /   /

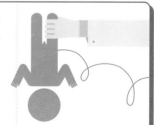

It is recommended that users bond with the baby shortly after delivery. Often, this bond will develop instantaneously. In other cases, the baby and the user will require a little more time. No two baby models are alike, and there is no right or wrong way for bonding to occur.

DATE ☐☐ / ☐☐ / ☐☐ through ☐☐ / ☐☐ / ☐☐

Always wash your hands before handling the baby. Human skin contains bacteria that, when transferred to the baby, can cause him to function improperly. If you do not have access to soap and water, disinfect your hands with a baby wipe or an alcohol-based hand sanitizer.

The baby's audio output system includes two lungs, vocal cords, and a mouth. The baby will use these features to communicate. Since most models do not come with verbal language facility pre-installed, your model's first attempts at communication may sound meaningless. These audio cues, called cries, actually contain a great deal of information for users.

DATE ☐☐ / ☐☐ / ☐☐ through ☐☐ / ☐☐ / ☐☐

The baby comes pre-loaded with the instincts and skills to begin breastfeeding almost immediately. The baby owner can choose to breastfeed or not, according to preference.

DATE ☐☐ / ☐☐ / ☐☐ through ☐☐ / ☐☐ / ☐☐

Swaddling consists of snugly wrapping the baby in a blanket. Your model might appear soothed by feelings of warmth and security, or frustrated by her sudden lack of mobility.

OVERALL SPECIFICATIONS

Weight	Length

THE HEAD

Circumference

HAIR

Color					Quantity	Texture
○ black	○ blond	○ brown	○ red			

Other comments

Note: If the baby has no hair (referred to as "bald"), note this in the record. Hair will appear eventually.

EYES

Color					Note any changes since birth
○ blue	○ brown	○ gray	○ green	○ hazel	

The baby recognizes the sight of his user(s).	○ yes	○ no
The baby smiles in response to seeing her user(s).	○ yes	○ no
The baby is interested in more complicated visual patterns.	○ yes	○ no

EARS

The baby recognizes the voice of her user(s).	○ yes	○ no
The baby turns his head in response to a sound.	○ yes	○ no

continues on following page

MONTHS

MAINTENANCE CHECKLIST

MOUTH

The baby smiles in response to hearing or seeing his user(s). ○ yes ○ no

Note: Smiles at this age are often the result of gas. Burp model and see if smile persists.

VOCAL CORDS

The baby makes noises other than crying. ○ yes ○ no

What are they?

HEAD/NECK

The baby has increased head control. ○ yes ○ no

Time when the baby began holding up her head by herself.

THE BODY

Skin condition	Overall complexion	Irregularities

Record and describe any skin conditions, such as cradle cap or baby acne, and how the condition has changed over the past three months.

Favorite place to nuzzle and kiss the baby.

ARMS/HANDS/FINGERS

How is the baby's coordination changing?

The baby reaches toward or grabs objects more often.	○ yes	○ no
The baby's fingers provide her with a constant source of entertainment.	○ yes	○ no

LEGS/FEET/TOES

The baby straightens out her legs and kicks.	○ yes	○ no
The baby bears some of his own weight when held in a standing position.	○ yes	○ no

SLEEP

The baby sleeps in longer blocks of time. (See page 86 for Baby's Sleep Chart.)	○ yes	○ no

CONSUMPTION

How much does the baby eat, on average, in a feeding?

How often does the baby feed? (See page 84 for Feeding Record.)

OTHER MILESTONES

Baby's first smile.

☐☐ / ☐☐ / ☐☐☐☐
Day   Month   Year

Feeding a baby using a bottle is a convenient and easy technique for many users. Users who do not breastfeed can feed the baby formula from this convenient receptacle. Those who do breastfeed can express the milk, which then can be served to the baby by people other than the mother.

WEEK **16**

DATE ☐☐ / ☐☐ / ☐☐ through ☐☐ / ☐☐ / ☐☐

If the baby has an unpleasant odor or begins crying for no apparent reason, his diaper may need to be reinstalled. With practice, the user will begin to ascertain a diaper's status simply by touching it and feeling for additional weight.

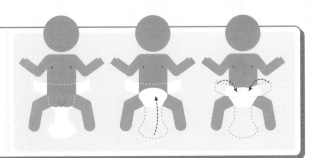

Frequent play time will benefit all models. It serves a tri-fold purpose: It makes the baby happy, can activate sleep mode, and teaches the baby about his relationship with the world. Find time to play games often.

DATE ☐☐ / ☐☐ / ☐☐ through ☐☐ / ☐☐ / ☐☐

Whenever the baby eats, he will swallow air. This air may lead to false feelings of fullness, uncomfortable gas, or the urge to spit up. The user can prevent these consequences by regularly burping the baby.

During the baby's first few months, sleep cycles follow a distinct pattern. First, the baby will experience Rapid Eye Movement (REM) sleep, then non-REM sleep. After a few months, the baby's sleep system will reverse, and non-REM will precede REM. Familiarize yourself with these cycles so you can understand the baby's sleep patterns.

When the baby is sitting up on his own, chewing or biting on objects, and has doubled his birth weight, he may be ready to consume solid food. This usually occurs between the baby's fourth and sixth months. Contact the baby's service provider before introducing the baby to solid food.

All models have a tendency to become soiled and should be cleaned regularly. When the baby is still small, give a sponge or basin bath. Never leave the baby unattended in a basin.

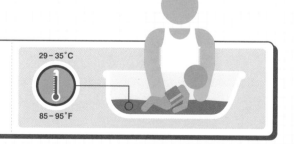

29 – 35˚C

85 – 95˚F

OVERALL SPECIFICATIONS

Weight

Length

THE HEAD

Circumference

HAIR

Color ○ ○ ○ ○
black   blond   brown   red

Quantity

Texture

Other comments

Note: If baldness persists, do not bring to service provider for repair. This condition will resolve itself eventually.

EYES | Baby eye color often changes during the first year.

Color ○ ○ ○ ○ ○
blue   brown   gray   green   hazel

Note any changes

The baby recognizes the sight of his user(s).	○ yes	○ no
The baby smiles in response to seeing her user(s).	○ yes	○ no
The baby is interested in more complicated visual patterns.	○ yes	○ no
The baby focuses on small objects.	○ yes	○ no

EARS

The baby recognizes the voice of her user(s).	○ yes	○ no
The baby turns his head in response to a sound.	○ yes	○ no

continues on following page

MAINTENANCE CHECKLIST

MOUTH

The baby smiles in response to hearing or seeing his user(s).	( ) yes	( ) no
The baby frequently gnaws on objects.	( ) yes	( ) no
The baby repeats and babbles simple sounds made by the user(s).	( ) yes	( ) no
The baby's favorite sounds.		
The baby makes pleasing sounds such as "mama" or "dada."	( ) yes	( ) no

HEAD/NECK   The baby has increased head control.   ( ) yes   ( ) no

THE BODY

Skin condition	Overall complexion	Irregularities

Record and describe any skin conditions, such as cradle cap or baby acne, and how the condition has changed over the last three months.

BODY MOVEMENT

The baby attempts to roll over. ( ) yes ( ) no	Date the baby first rolled over. [ ][ ] / [ ][ ] / [ ][ ][ ][ ] Day Month Year

The baby sits (with help from his user[s]).   ( ) yes   ( ) no

ARMS/HANDS/FINGERS

The baby reaches toward or grabs objects more often.	( ) yes	( ) no
While on her stomach, the baby supports her upper body with her arms extended.	( ) yes	( ) no

LEGS/FEET/TOES

The baby bears some of his own weight when held in a standing position.	○ yes	○ no
The baby pushes into a standing position.	○ yes	○ no

SLEEP

The baby sleeps in longer blocks of time. (See page 86 for Baby's Sleep Chart.)	○ yes	○ no
The user sleeps in longer blocks of time.	○ yes	○ no

CONSUMPTION

	Formula/breast milk	Solids
How much does the baby eat, on average, in a feeding?		

How often does the baby feed? (See page 84 for Feeding Record.)

What are the baby's favorite foods?

What foods does the baby dislike?

Signs of allergic reaction to any foods.

OTHER MILESTONES

Your model is programmed to sit unassisted (just as it will eventually walk, talk, and drive of its own power).

Has this feature begun to function yet? ○ yes ○ no	Date the baby first sat unassisted.

Date the baby first sat unassisted.

[ ][ ] / [ ][ ] / [ ][ ][ ][ ]
Day   Month   Year

 **WARNING SIGNS:** If any parts or functions are missing or not working in the expected manner, contact the baby's service provider immediately.

DATE ☐☐ / ☐☐ / ☐☐ through ☐☐ / ☐☐ / ☐☐

By six months, the baby will realize she has a pre-programmed ability to speak in your language. Talking to the baby will acti-vate this realization. Initially, she will learn to repeat sounds you make and will eventually learn to speak herself.

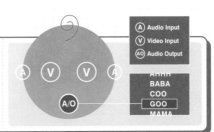

(A) Audio Input
(V) Video Input
(A/O) Audio Output

AHHH
BABA
COO
GOO
MAMA

The baby comes pre-installed with a pincer grasp that enables the baby to automatically feed himself. This grasp requires at least twelve months to become fully functional. Practice self-feeding exercises with the baby to prepare him for this independent function.

DATE ☐☐ / ☐☐ / ☐☐ through ☐☐ / ☐☐ / ☐☐

WEEK 30

DATE ☐☐ / ☐☐ / ☐☐ through ☐☐ / ☐☐ / ☐☐

During the baby's first year of life, you will need to reinstall diapers numerous times a day. Although many users find this process tedious, the benefits far outweigh the inconvenience. Having the proper supplies on hand makes the process easier.

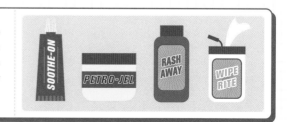

The use of certain accessories called clothing will protect the baby from direct sunlight, moisture, cold, scratches, dust, and other common hazards. These accessories may be purchased at any number of specialty retailers.

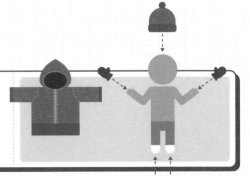

DATE ☐☐ / ☐☐ / ☐☐ through ☐☐ / ☐☐ / ☐☐

To guarantee quality performance, each model should be cleaned after every two or three days of use. Give a bathtub bath to models that are more than six months old.

DATE ☐☐ / ☐☐ / ☐☐ through ☐☐ / ☐☐ / ☐☐

The baby might come pre-programmed with cues that indicate he is readying to enter sleep mode. These include rubbing his eyes or pulling at his ears. If you see these signs, quickly work to activate sleep mode. If you do not, the baby may become overstimulated and sleep mode will be delayed indefinitely.

DATE ☐☐ / ☐☐ / ☐☐ through ☐☐ / ☐☐ / ☐☐

WEEK 38

DATE ☐☐ / ☐☐ / ☐☐ through ☐☐ / ☐☐ / ☐☐

OVERALL SPECIFICATIONS

Weight

Length

THE HEAD

Circumference

HAIR

Color ○ ○ ○ ○
black   blond   brown   red

Quantity

Texture

Other comments

EYES | The baby's eyes may still change color.

Color ○ ○ ○ ○ ○
blue   brown   gray   green   hazel

Note any changes

The baby is interested in complicated visual patterns.	○ yes	○ no
The baby focuses on small objects.	○ yes	○ no
The baby tracks moving objects with her eyes.	○ yes	○ no
The baby's distance vision is improving.	○ yes	○ no

EARS

The baby recognizes the voice of her user(s).	○ yes	○ no
The baby responds to loud sounds.	○ yes	○ no

continues on following page

MAINTENANCE CHECKLIST

MOUTH

The baby smiles in response to hearing or seeing his user(s).	◯ yes ◯ no
The baby frequently gnaws on objects.	◯ yes ◯ no
The baby tries to imitate the user(s) by babbling.	◯ yes ◯ no
The baby makes pleasing sounds, such as "mama" or "dada."	◯ yes ◯ no

Date when the baby said "mama." ☐☐ / ☐☐ / ☐☐☐☐
                                       Day   Month   Year

Date when the baby said "dada." ☐☐ / ☐☐ / ☐☐☐☐
                                       Day   Month   Year

BRAIN | Now you may begin to see evidence of how the baby is thinking.

When you move a toy out of sight, the baby looks for it.	◯ yes ◯ no

PSYCHOLOGY | Separation anxiety may set in at this time.

The baby becomes upset when you say good-bye and leave.	◯ yes ◯ no

THE BODY

Skin condition	Overall complexion	Irregularities

BODY MOVEMENT

The baby attempts to roll over.	◯ yes	◯ no

Date the baby first rolled over.   ☐☐ / ☐☐ / ☐☐☐☐
                                    Day   Month   Year

The baby sits (with help from his user[s]).	◯ yes	◯ no
The baby sees an object and reaches for it.	◯ yes	◯ no
The baby can pass an object from hand to hand.	◯ yes	◯ no

ARMS/HANDS/FINGERS

The baby reaches toward or grabs objects.	◯ yes	◯ no
The baby manipulates and is learning how objects work.	◯ yes	◯ no
The baby waves hello and goodbye.	◯ yes	◯ no
The baby has a developed pincer movement, enabling her to pick up small objects with thumb and forefinger.	◯ yes	◯ no

LEGS/FEET/TOES

The baby moves more independently, learning to crawl and/or pull up.	◯ yes	◯ no
The baby cruises (walks while holding furniture or a walking toy).	◯ yes	◯ no

continues on following page

MONTHS

MAINTENANCE CHECKLIST

SLEEP

The baby sleeps in a regular nighttime pattern. (See page 86 for Baby's Sleep Chart.) ◯ yes ◯ no

The baby sleeps for more than six hours at a time. ◯ yes ◯ no

Date when the baby first slept for
more than six hours. [ ] / [ ] / [   ]
Day Month Year

The user sleeps for more than six hours at a time. ◯ yes ◯ no

Date when the user first slept for more
than six hours. [ ] / [ ] / [   ]
Day Month Year

CONSUMPTION

How much does the baby eat, on average, in a feeding?	Formula/breast milk	Solids

How often does the baby feed? (See page 84 for Feeding Record.)

What are the baby's new favorite foods?

What new foods does the baby dislike?

Signs of allergic reaction to specific foods.

The baby picks up food and feeds herself. ◯ yes ◯ no

OTHER MILESTONES

The baby sits unassisted. ◯ yes ◯ no

DATE ☐☐ / ☐☐ / ☐☐ through ☐☐ / ☐☐ / ☐☐

Many service providers believe that massage can strengthen the immune system, improve muscle development, and stimulate growth of the baby. Massage has a calming effect on most models and allows the user and baby to develop a closer bond.

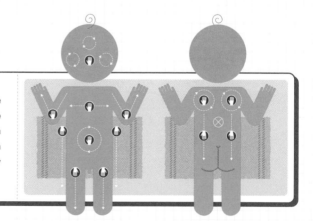

DATE ☐☐ / ☐☐ / ☐☐ through ☐☐ / ☐☐ / ☐☐

As the baby becomes more mobile, after nine months of age, she is liable to begin exploring her surroundings. Ensure that your model remains safe by childproofing the home.

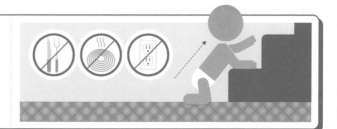

DATE ☐☐ / ☐☐ / ☐☐ through ☐☐ / ☐☐ / ☐☐

Music is highly recommended during play; it can teach the baby the basics of rhythm, movement, and vocalization, hastening the baby's intellectual and creative development.

DATE ☐☐ / ☐☐ / ☐☐ through ☐☐ / ☐☐ / ☐☐

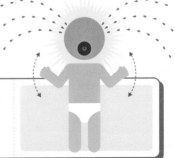

As the baby begins to understand his world, he might become frustrated when trying to communicate what he wants. This frustration often manifests itself in the form of tantrums. Focus on positive reinforcement and be patient.

The baby will begin to crawl, pull up, and even walk. All models develop some form of pre-walking mobility, whether crawling, scooting, or sliding. Stay nearby and provide support.

WEEK 51

During the first year, some users shorten the baby's hair. Do so carefully and with the proper tools to avoid damaging the baby. If the hair does not grow back immediately, do not be alarmed. Hair grows more regularly as the baby ages.

 **MONTHS**

OVERALL SPECIFICATIONS

Weight	Length

THE HEAD

Circumference

HAIR

Color ○ ○ ○ ○
black blond brown red

Quantity

Texture

Other comments

EYES

Color ○ ○ ○ ○ ○
blue brown gray green hazel

The baby focuses on small objects. ○ yes ○ no

The baby tracks moving objects with her eyes. ○ yes ○ no

The baby's distance vision is improving. ○ yes ○ no

EARS

The baby recognizes the voice of her user(s). ○ yes ○ no

The baby responds to loud sounds. ○ yes ○ no

MOUTH

The baby tries to imitate the user(s) by babbling. ○ yes ○ no

The baby makes pleasing sounds, such as "mama" or "dada." ○ yes ○ no

Date when the baby said "mama."

☐☐ / ☐☐ / ☐☐☐☐
Day   Month   Year

Date when the baby said "dada."

☐☐ / ☐☐ / ☐☐☐☐
Day   Month   Year

The baby says some words with clarity. ○ yes ○ no

HEAD

The baby shakes her head "no."	◯ yes	◯ no

BRAIN

When you move a toy out of sight, the baby looks for it.	◯ yes	◯ no
When a user names an object, the baby looks for and finds it.	◯ yes	◯ no

PSYCHOLOGY

The baby becomes upset when you say goodbye and leave.	◯ yes	◯ no
The baby responds when you say "no."	◯ yes	◯ no

THE BODY

Skin condition	Overall complexion	Irregularities

BODY MOVEMENT

The baby attempts to roll over.	◯ yes ◯ no	Date the baby first rolled over. [ ][ ] / [ ][ ] / [ ][ ][ ] Day Month Year
The baby sits (with help from his user[s]).	◯ yes ◯ no	The baby finds the user(s) when called from another room. ◯ yes ◯ no
The baby moves more independently, learning to walk and climb.		◯ yes ◯ no

continues on following page

 **MONTHS**

ARMS/HANDS/FINGERS

The baby manipulates and is learning how objects work.	◯ yes	◯ no
The baby waves hello and goodbye.	◯ yes	◯ no
The baby has a developed pincer movement, enabling him to pick up small objects with thumb and forefinger.	◯ yes	◯ no
The baby can pass an object from hand to hand.	◯ yes	◯ no
The baby points where she wants to go.	◯ yes	◯ no
The baby places objects in a container.	◯ yes	◯ no

LEGS/FEET/TOES

The baby bears some of his own weight when held in a standing position.	◯ yes	◯ no
The baby pushes into a standing position.	◯ yes	◯ no
The baby moves more independently, learning to crawl and/or pull up.	◯ yes	◯ no
The baby cruises (walks while holding furniture or a walking toy).	◯ yes	◯ no

The baby's favorite mode of transportation.

SLEEP

The baby sleeps in a regular nighttime pattern. (See page 86 for Baby's Sleep Chart.)	◯ yes	◯ no
The baby sleeps for more than six hours at a time.	◯ yes	◯ no

Date when the baby first slept for more than six hours.

☐☐ / ☐☐ / ☐☐☐☐
Day   Month   Year

The user sleeps for more than six hours at a time.	◯ yes	◯ no

Date when the user first slept for more than six hours.

☐☐ / ☐☐ / ☐☐☐☐
Day   Month   Year

CONSUMPTION

How much does the baby eat, on average, in a feeding?	Formula/breast milk	Solids

How often does the baby feed? (See page 84 for Feeding Record.)

What are the baby's new favorite foods?

What new foods does the baby dislike?

Signs of allergic reaction to specific foods.

The baby picks up food and feeds herself.	◯ yes	◯ no

 **WARNING SIGNS:** If any parts or functions are missing or not working in the expected manner, contact the baby's service provider immediately.

Baby Bladder Function

DAY	MONTH	DATE	# OF BLADDER FUNCTIONS
SUN			
MON			
TUE			
WED			
THUR			
FRI			
SAT			
SUN			
MON			
TUE			
WED			
THUR			
FRI			
SAT			
SUN			
MON			
TUE			
WED			
THUR			
FRI			
SAT			

DAY	MONTH	DATE	# OF BLADDER FUNCTIONS
SUN			
MON			
TUE			
WED			
THUR			
FRI			
SAT			
SUN			
MON			
TUE			
WED			
THUR			
FRI			
SAT			
SUN			
MON			
TUE			
WED			
THUR			
FRI			
SAT			

Baby Bowel Function

DATE	TIME	COLOR	CONSISTENCY	DELIVERY
				○ easy ○ difficult
				○ easy ○ difficult
				○ easy ○ difficult
				○ easy ○ difficult
				○ easy ○ difficult
				○ easy ○ difficult
				○ easy ○ difficult
				○ easy ○ difficult
				○ easy ○ difficult
				○ easy ○ difficult
				○ easy ○ difficult
				○ easy ○ difficult
				○ easy ○ difficult
				○ easy ○ difficult
				○ easy ○ difficult
				○ easy ○ difficult
				○ easy ○ difficult
				○ easy ○ difficult
				○ easy ○ difficult
				○ easy ○ difficult
				○ easy ○ difficult
				○ easy ○ difficult

DATE	TIME	COLOR	CONSISTENCY	DELIVERY
				○ easy ○ difficult
				○ easy ○ difficult
				○ easy ○ difficult
				○ easy ○ difficult
				○ easy ○ difficult
				○ easy ○ difficult
				○ easy ○ difficult
				○ easy ○ difficult
				○ easy ○ difficult
				○ easy ○ difficult
				○ easy ○ difficult
				○ easy ○ difficult
				○ easy ○ difficult
				○ easy ○ difficult
				○ easy ○ difficult
				○ easy ○ difficult
				○ easy ○ difficult
				○ easy ○ difficult
				○ easy ○ difficult
				○ easy ○ difficult
				○ easy ○ difficult

Feeding Record

DATE	TIME STARTED	SIDE STARTED ON	MINUTES AT BREAST
		◯ LEFT ◯ RIGHT	LEFT: RIGHT:
		◯ LEFT ◯ RIGHT	LEFT: RIGHT:
		◯ LEFT ◯ RIGHT	LEFT: RIGHT:
		◯ LEFT ◯ RIGHT	LEFT: RIGHT:
		◯ LEFT ◯ RIGHT	LEFT: RIGHT:
		◯ LEFT ◯ RIGHT	LEFT: RIGHT:
		◯ LEFT ◯ RIGHT	LEFT: RIGHT:
		◯ LEFT ◯ RIGHT	LEFT: RIGHT:
		◯ LEFT ◯ RIGHT	LEFT: RIGHT:
		◯ LEFT ◯ RIGHT	LEFT: RIGHT:
		◯ LEFT ◯ RIGHT	LEFT: RIGHT:
		◯ LEFT ◯ RIGHT	LEFT: RIGHT:
		◯ LEFT ◯ RIGHT	LEFT: RIGHT:
		◯ LEFT ◯ RIGHT	LEFT: RIGHT:
		◯ LEFT ◯ RIGHT	LEFT: RIGHT:
		◯ LEFT ◯ RIGHT	LEFT: RIGHT:
		◯ LEFT ◯ RIGHT	LEFT: RIGHT:
		◯ LEFT ◯ RIGHT	LEFT: RIGHT:
		◯ LEFT ◯ RIGHT	LEFT: RIGHT:
		◯ LEFT ◯ RIGHT	LEFT: RIGHT:
		◯ LEFT ◯ RIGHT	LEFT: RIGHT:
		◯ LEFT ◯ RIGHT	LEFT: RIGHT:

DATE	TIME STARTED	SIDE STARTED ON	MINUTES AT BREAST
		○ LEFT ○ RIGHT	LEFT: _____ RIGHT: _____
		○ LEFT ○ RIGHT	LEFT: _____ RIGHT: _____
		○ LEFT ○ RIGHT	LEFT: _____ RIGHT: _____
		○ LEFT ○ RIGHT	LEFT: _____ RIGHT: _____
		○ LEFT ○ RIGHT	LEFT: _____ RIGHT: _____
		○ LEFT ○ RIGHT	LEFT: _____ RIGHT: _____
		○ LEFT ○ RIGHT	LEFT: _____ RIGHT: _____
		○ LEFT ○ RIGHT	LEFT: _____ RIGHT: _____
		○ LEFT ○ RIGHT	LEFT: _____ RIGHT: _____
		○ LEFT ○ RIGHT	LEFT: _____ RIGHT: _____
		○ LEFT ○ RIGHT	LEFT: _____ RIGHT: _____
		○ LEFT ○ RIGHT	LEFT: _____ RIGHT: _____
		○ LEFT ○ RIGHT	LEFT: _____ RIGHT: _____
		○ LEFT ○ RIGHT	LEFT: _____ RIGHT: _____
		○ LEFT ○ RIGHT	LEFT: _____ RIGHT: _____
		○ LEFT ○ RIGHT	LEFT: _____ RIGHT: _____
		○ LEFT ○ RIGHT	LEFT: _____ RIGHT: _____
		○ LEFT ○ RIGHT	LEFT: _____ RIGHT: _____
		○ LEFT ○ RIGHT	LEFT: _____ RIGHT: _____
		○ LEFT ○ RIGHT	LEFT: _____ RIGHT: _____
		○ LEFT ○ RIGHT	LEFT: _____ RIGHT: _____

BABY'S SLEEP CHART

zzz	SUN	MON	TUE	WED	THUR	FRI	SAT	SUN	MON	TUE	WED	THUR	FRI	SAT
11:30 P.M.														
11:00 P.M.														
10:30 P.M.														
10:00 P.M.														
09:30 P.M.														
09:00 P.M.														
08:30 P.M.														
08:00 P.M.														
07:30 P.M.														
07:00 P.M.														
06:30 P.M.														
06:00 P.M.														
05:30 P.M.														
05:00 P.M.														
04:30 P.M.														
04:00 P.M.														
03:30 P.M.														
03:00 P.M.														
02:30 P.M.														
02:00 P.M.														
01:30 P.M.														
01:00 P.M.														
12:30 P.M.														
12:00 P.M.														
11:30 A.M.														
11:00 A.M.														
10:30 A.M.														
10:00 A.M.														
09:30 A.M.														
09:00 A.M.														
08:30 A.M.														
08:00 A.M.														
07:30 A.M.														
07:00 A.M.														
06:30 A.M.														
06:00 A.M.														
05:30 A.M.														
05:00 A.M.														
04:30 A.M.														
04:00 A.M.														
03:30 A.M.														
03:00 A.M.														
02:30 A.M.														
02:00 A.M.														
01:30 A.M.														
01:00 A.M.														
12:30 A.M.														
12:00 A.M.														

	SUN	MON	TUE	WED	THUR	FRI	SAT	SUN	MON	TUE	WED	THUR	FRI	SAT
11:30 P.M.														
11:00 P.M.														
10:30 P.M.														
10:00 P.M.														
09:30 P.M.														
09:00 P.M.														
08:30 P.M.														
08:00 P.M.														
07:30 P.M.														
07:00 P.M.														
06:30 P.M.														
06:00 P.M.														
05:30 P.M.														
05:00 P.M.														
04:30 P.M.														
04:00 P.M.														
03:30 P.M.														
03:00 P.M.														
02:30 P.M.														
02:00 P.M.														
01:30 P.M.														
01:00 P.M.														
12:30 P.M.														
12:00 P.M.														
11:30 A.M.														
11:00 A.M.														
10:30 A.M.														
10:00 A.M.														
09:30 A.M.														
09:00 A.M.														
08:30 A.M.														
08:00 A.M.														
07:30 A.M.														
07:00 A.M.														
06:30 A.M.														
06:00 A.M.														
05:30 A.M.														
05:00 A.M.														
04:30 A.M.														
04:00 A.M.														
03:30 A.M.														
03:00 A.M.														
02:30 A.M.														
02:00 A.M.														
01:30 A.M.														
01:00 A.M.														
12:30 A.M.														
12:00 A.M.														

Service Records

Your model will require periodic visits to the service provider for routine check-ups. It is also recommended that the baby be brought to see the provider in the case of any unusual or puzzling symptoms. If in doubt, always call your service provider with questions. Make notes during each visit on the convenient Service Record charts on the pages that follow.

PRIMARY SERVICE PROVIDER

Name

Address

Phone Number

OTHER AUTHORIZED SERVICE PROVIDERS

Name

Address

Phone Number

Name

Address

Phone Number

OTHER INFORMATION

Emergency numbers

Allergies

Blood type   ◯   ◯   ◯   ◯   Rh factor   ◯   ◯
          A   B   AB   O   +   −

SERVICE RECORD

Date of visit.

	/		/		
Day		Month		Year	

Service provider seen.

Reason for visit.

Weight	Height	Immunizations

Other diagnoses.

Medications prescribed, if any.

SERVICE RECORD

Date of visit.

	/		/		
Day		Month		Year	

Service provider seen.

Reason for visit.

Weight	Height	Immunizations

Other diagnoses.

Medications prescribed, if any.

Service Records

SERVICE RECORD

| Date of visit. | □□ / □□ / □□□□ |
| | Day   Month   Year |

Service provider seen.

Reason for visit.

| Weight | Height | Immunizations |

Other diagnoses.

Medications prescribed, if any.

SERVICE RECORD

| Date of visit. | □□ / □□ / □□□□ |
| | Day   Month   Year |

Service provider seen.

Reason for visit.

| Weight | Height | Immunizations |

Other diagnoses.

Medications prescribed, if any.

SERVICE RECORD

Date of visit.				/			/			
		Day			Month			Year		

Service provider seen.

Reason for visit.

Weight	Height	Immunizations

Other diagnoses.

Medications prescribed, if any.

SERVICE RECORD

Date of visit.				/			/			
		Day			Month			Year		

Service provider seen.

Reason for visit.

Weight	Height	Immunizations

Other diagnoses.

Medications prescribed, if any.

Service Records

SERVICE RECORD

Date of visit. ☐☐ / ☐☐ / ☐☐☐☐

Day   Month   Year

Service provider seen.

Reason for visit.

Weight | **Height** | **Immunizations**

Other diagnoses.

Medications prescribed, if any.

SERVICE RECORD

Date of visit. ☐☐ / ☐☐ / ☐☐☐☐

Day   Month   Year

Service provider seen.

Reason for visit.

Weight | **Height** | **Immunizations**

Other diagnoses.

Medications prescribed, if any.

SERVICE RECORD

Date of visit.

Day	Month	Year

Service provider seen.

Reason for visit.

Weight	Height	Immunizations

Other diagnoses.

Medications prescribed, if any.

SERVICE RECORD

Date of visit.

Day	Month	Year

Service provider seen.

Reason for visit.

Weight	Height	Immunizations

Other diagnoses.

Medications prescribed, if any.

Service Records

SERVICE RECORD

Date of visit.			/			/				
		Day			Month			Year		

Service provider seen.

Reason for visit.

Weight	Height	Immunizations

Other diagnoses.

Medications prescribed, if any.

SERVICE RECORD

Date of visit.			/			/				
		Day			Month			Year		

Service provider seen.

Reason for visit.

Weight	Height	Immunizations

Other diagnoses.

Medications prescribed, if any.

SERVICE RECORD

Date of visit.

Day	Month	Year

Service provider seen.

Reason for visit.

Weight | Height | Immunizations

Other diagnoses.

Medications prescribed, if any.

SERVICE RECORD

Date of visit.

Day	Month	Year

Service provider seen.

Reason for visit.

Weight | Height | Immunizations

Other diagnoses.

Medications prescribed, if any.

Assembling a Baby First-Aid Kit

All users should create a first-aid kit containing tools, patches, and accessories designed to treat the baby in the event of an emergency. Some users will create one kit for the home, another for the car, and a portable kit to use while traveling. The kits should be readily accessible but out of the baby's reach. It is recommended that you check the kit monthly to replace any expired medications or outdated supplies. Purchase a plastic bin for the small items and keep large items nearby.

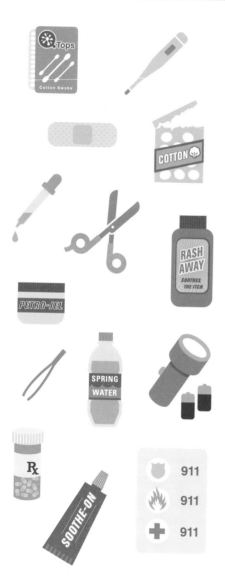

The first-aid kit should contain

❑ Sterile gauze bandages and strips
❑ Cotton balls
❑ Cotton swabs
❑ Adhesive bandages
❑ Surgical tape
❑ Digital thermometer
❑ Scissors
❑ Tweezers
❑ Medicine dropper or dispenser
❑ Flashlight with extra batteries
❑ Extra blanket
❑ Antiseptic cream
❑ Antibiotic ointment
❑ Calamine lotion
❑ PABA-free sunscreen (15 SPF or higher)
❑ Burn spray or ointment
❑ Hydrocortisone cream (1% or less)
❑ Petroleum jelly
❑ Soap
❑ Bottle of clean water
❑ Ibuprofen or acetaminophen
❑ Diphenhydramine or other antihistamine
❑ Decongestants
❑ Cough suppressants
❑ Other medications specific to your model's health
❑ CPR and Heimlich maneuver instruction card or manual
❑ Ipecac or poison kit
❑ List of emergency phone numbers
❑ Sterile hand wipes